NOW THEN AGAIN

Penny Penniston

BROADWAY PLAY PUBLISHING INC
224 E 62nd St, NY, NY 10065
www.broadwayplaypub.com
info@broadwayplaypub.com

NOW THEN AGAIN

First published by B P P I in October 2001
First printing, this edition: June 2014
I S B N: 978-0-88145-602-8

Book design: Marie Donovan
Page make-up: Adobe Indesign
Typeface: Palatino
Copy editing: Sue Gilad
Printed and bound in the U S A

NOW THEN AGAIN had its first production with Bailiwick Repertory in Chicago, Illinois on 17 February 2000. The original cast and creative contributors were:

HENRY ....Joseph Wycoff
DR TROUSANT...Casey Hayes
FELIX ....Richard Cotovsky
GINNY.. Katie Mclean
CHRIS .... Benjamin Shields
MINISTER/RABBI/MUSICIAN........................ Bill McGough

Director...Jeremy Wechsler
Scenic design...Susan Kaip
Lighting design ....Michael Rourke
Video design..................... Kim Hassenfeld & Chuck Jones
Sound design/original music ....Joseph Fosco
Costume design..Karen Krolak
Technical direction... Dan Griffiths
Physics consultants ...... John G Cramer & Morris Binkley
Stage manager..Kristy Kambanis

AKNOWLEDGMENTS

Thanks to all the people who helped this script
along its way: John G Cramer for the inspiration and
assistance; Morris Binkley, who corrected my physics,
checked my math and raided Fermilab for props;
David Zak and Bailiwick Repertory; the original
cast and crew; John Gribbin; Meridith Rentz; Bill
Dorland, Dr J T Penniston; the Thursday night gang
at the Screenwriter's Group; and Fermilab National
Accelerator Laboratory.

For (and with) Jeremy

INTRODUCTION

Quantum mechanics, the physics theory of matter and energy at the smallest distance and energy scales, is a very weird theory indeed. It tells us of waves that spread out in all directions, then abruptly disappear like a pricked balloon when a measurement is made. It tells us of cats that are half alive and half dead until we look at them. It tells us of particles that can pass simultaneously through two holes, then reassemble themselves. It tells us of measurements separated by many miles that can reach across space-time to influence each other. It tells us of objects that can be viewed with light, without a single photon of light actually interacting with the object. The weirdness and paradoxes of quantum mechanics are a scandal that is a growing part of our popular culture.

Physics theories normally begin with an underlying vision of how the universe works, then build on this visual foundation with mathematics. Quantum mechanics, however, was a mathematical formalism that leaped full-grown from the heads of Schrödinger and Heisenberg without the preliminary of an underlying physical picture. Since that time more than seventy years ago, physicists and philosophers have been debating about what the underlying mechanisms behind quantum mechanics may be. Today there is no consensus.

The missing physical vision is supplied by the *Transactional Interpretation of Quantum Mechanics*, which I published in 1986. it takes the psi-star part of the quantum formalism quite literally as a backwards-in-time wave; it depicts quantum events as a handshake between the future and the past through the medium of quantum waves that travel in both time directions. It thereby resolves *all* of the quantum paradoxes in a simple and economical way, without doing violence to cause-and-effect or relativity. (See John Gribbin's *Schrödinger's Kittens and the Search for Reality* and the original transactional interpretation paper at http:// www.npl.washington.edu/ti for more information.)

Penny Penniston's new play, NOW THEN AGAIN, weaves this transactional handshake mechanism into a metaphor that is the basis for an appealing love story. The future interacts with the past; nature explores alternatives until it resolves them with a buildup to the final transaction. Of course, in a real macroscopic world, this is not actually how things work, but at the quantum scale the play is a nice map for thinking about the probings and development of a transaction that ultimately becomes an element of reality.

I find Penny's work quite remarkable. It transports cutting-edge physics to the stage, to tell a story that could not be told in any other way. It's perhaps the most enjoyable medium I've seen for learning how the universe might work at the quantum level. I hope you enjoy it too.

John G Cramer
Seattle, Washington

ACT ONE

NOW

(Fermilab National Accelerator Laboratory in Batavia, Illinois. Among the playing areas: HENRY's *office—an insanely cluttered little corner;* GINNY's *office—a small tidy cubicle; also—a hallway with a burnt-out light bulb. In* GINNY's *office: A radio on the desk plays violin music, loudly. A framed photograph of handsome, twenty-eight year-old* CHRIS PRESTON *sits prominently on the desk.* HENRY RAINER, *twenty-seven, hides in the small space under the desk. He stares at a note pad in his lap.* HENRY *is wearing whatever happened to be in the front of his closet that morning. Now and always,* HENRY *is completely absorbed in the work. He doesn't notice his cramped quarters. He doesn't notice the violin music that plays from the radio on the desk. The angry voice of* DR ARMAND TROUSANT *thunders onto the stage.)*

TROUSANT: *(O S)* Henry!

*(*HENRY *doesn't answer. He has tuned out everything except the note pad. It's as if he were waiting for it to speak.* TROUSANT *enters.)*

TROUSANT: Henry?!

(No answer)

TROUSANT: Listen you little nuisance. I have poked through every closet in the building. It's a very big building—

(As TROUSANT *approaches the cubicle, he sees* HENRY *hiding. He yanks the desk chair away.)*

TROUSANT: Henry!

HENRY: *(Staring at the equations)* Shhhhhhhhhhh.

*(*TROUSANT *rips the cord to the radio out of the wall. The violin music stops.)*

HENRY: Damn.

TROUSANT: You know, I am a very relaxed peaceful guy. I do yoga, I drink wine, I'm a member of Oprah's book club. Really it is only a lifetime spent getting in touch with my sensitive side that keeps me from taking this radio and squashing you like a grape! *(He bangs the radio on the desk.)*

HENRY: This isn't actually my desk.

TROUSANT: Oh.

HENRY: Experimental projects. I thought it'd be the last place you'd look.

TROUSANT: Yes, thank you. It was.

HENRY: Forty-eight minutes. You're faster than Doctor Binkley.

TROUSANT: Henry, twenty-five scientists are in the auditorium right now waiting to hear a presentation from you. Since they do, of course, make recommendations about your funding, I was hoping you might show up.

HENRY: Twenty-five. Way too many.

TROUSANT: No. I counted myself. Twenty-five. I have a Nobel Prize, you know.

HENRY: Glossophobia.

TROUSANT: Do not start with me today—

HENRY: Fear of speaking in public. I can handle two people, maybe three, but definitely not four, so twenty-five—you can just forget it.

TROUSANT: You know, Henry, the department is beginning to think you don't exist. They think I made you up. You don't come to meetings, you don't answer your calls—

HENRY: I exist.

TROUSANT: Glad to hear it. Now get out from under the damn desk.

HENRY: Officially, I'm still hiding.

(*Reluctantly,* HENRY *pulls himself out from under the desk.* TROUSANT *notices the equations on* HENRY's *pad of paper.*)

TROUSANT: What is this?

HENRY: Well, it's math—

TROUSANT: You are supposed to be working on Lattice Gauge Calculations.

HENRY: I got distracted.

TROUSANT: You have a grant. You do remember the grant?

HENRY: It just wasn't speaking to me.

TROUSANT: I'm your boss. I speak to you.

HENRY: Let me tell you something, Armand: Weakly Interacting Massive Particles.

TROUSANT: Oh good God.

HENRY: O K, it's all hypothetical—I know. But theoretically—maybe—pretending that detector engineering was like—ten years more advanced, some versions of string theory predict—

TROUSANT: Henry, this is why they hate us—

HENRY: Who?

TROUSANT: Them. That run the lab. They've got a billion-dollar machine down there, whole rooms of computers, and you're up here deciding the structure of the universe with a pencil and paper.

HENRY: Mostly I use these green felt-tip pens—

TROUSANT: You can't just think about the things you want to think about. You have to think about the things they give you money to think about.

HENRY: It's speaking to me, Armand.

TROUSANT: Well, tell it to shut up. Right now, you've got people waiting. People who want to hear about the decay properties of heavy mesons.

HENRY: Twenty-five people.

TROUSANT: Let's go.

HENRY: Just give me a second alone.

TROUSANT: I spent all morning searching the building for you—I'm not letting you out of my sight.

HENRY: Glossophobia. I'm serious Armand. You go on.

(TROUSANT *doesn't move.*)

HENRY: You want me to get up there and throw up? Because I will. I'm nervous and if you don't give me a little time here, I'll throw up all over that German plasma physics guy that always sits in the front and grunts.

TROUSANT: Six minutes. I expect to see you at that podium in six minutes.

(*Reluctantly,* TROUSANT *leaves. Now alone,* HENRY *paces— nervous, anxious, working himself into a sweaty panic.*)

HENRY: Hide…hide…where can I hide? He'll check the closets…this time, the ladies' bathrooms are definitely out…

(HENRY *notices a large vent on one of the walls—a perfect hiding place. He pulls on the vent. A janitor,* FELIX, *fifty-four, enters; with shaggy hair and a beard, he looks little crazy.*)

FELIX: Henry!

HENRY: Felix, not now. I'm busy.

FELIX: It's after eight. We shouldn't be here. We should go.

HENRY: Not today. Today, I'm hiding.

FELIX: Every day. Every day between eight and nine o'clock. You never know when she'll come.

HENRY: Look, I don't have time for destiny tonight.

FELIX: But it's her.

HENRY: Felix, stop trying to set me up. I'm fine.

FELIX: Look at you—the air ducts? You don't think that's a little extravagant? O K, so you want to hide. But most people hide in closets, or under beds, or in far-away towns under assumed names—but you—you rip out dry wall.

(HENRY *tries to pry open the vent with office supplies. It doesn't work.*)

HENRY: Can you give me a hand here?

FELIX: Let's hide on the fourth floor under the burnt-out light bulb.

HENRY: Too risky. Open field. Lots of foot traffic.

FELIX: But it's her.

HENRY: Who, Felix? Who?

FELIX: I don't know, not exactly. All I know is that you will meet her under the burnt-out light between eight and nine o'clock.

HENRY: Are you all right? I mean, are you feeling all right?

FELIX: You're the one climbing into the walls.

HENRY: *(Checking his watch)* Shit! Three minutes.

FELIX: The woman of your destiny. You don't believe me.

HENRY: You did way too many drugs in the sixties. She's not real.

FELIX: I'm not interested in reality. I want possibilities.

(HENRY looks in frustration at the stubborn vent.)

HENRY: This isn't working, is it?

FELIX: Come on, come sit with me. The crazy janitor. Come sit.

(Defeated, HENRY grabs his bag. He and FELIX head out of the room.)

HENRY: You'll keep a lookout for Trousant?

FELIX: Yes. Right. I look out for you. You'll see.

(HENRY and FELIX leave.)

(Across the stage at a podium. GINNY ADEN, twenty-two, enters for a presentation. Her clothes are soft and feminine; a diamond engagement ring graces her left hand. She speaks with confidence and a perky Southern drawl.)

GINNY: Now, in Italy, the Gran Sasso Underground Laboratory is searching for WIMP dark matter using cryogenic detectors. CRESST has installed a new cold box made from radiopure copper and is conducting the first low background runs with four two-sixty-two gram sapphire detectors.

(GINNY's fiancé, CHRIS PRESTON, twenty-eight, sneaks in the back with a MINISTER. CHRIS is handsome in that preppy, clean cut, Southern kind of way.)

MINISTER: What's she talking about?

CHRIS: Does it matter? Look at her.

GINNY: The latest development is a method to measure simultaneously the phonons and the scintillation light produced by particle interactions in a scintillating crystal. This will significantly improve background discrimination and will increase the weakly interacting massive particle detection sensitivity.

MINISTER: Nice smile. Good hair.

CHRIS: I have loved her since I was nine years old.

MINISTER: That's sweet. Love. The church is in favor of it, you know. *(Looking at* GINNY*)* She looks smart.

CHRIS: She's smart.

MINISTER: No, but she looks really smart. A physicist. Are you that smart?

CHRIS: I'm a lawyer.

MINISTER: *(Disappointed)* Oh.

CHRIS: I graduated magna cum laude you know.

MINISTER: I'm sure you're very smart. *(Checking his watch)* You know, I do have the ladies' pot luck at nine-thirty.

CHRIS: She'll just be a minute.

(Polite applause as GINNY *steps down from the podium.)*

CHRIS: See? She's done. Go wait in her office. Don't let her see you.

(The MINISTER *leaves.* TROUSANT *steps up to the podium.)*

TROUSANT: Thank you. Now, we're going to turn the presentation over to the theoretical physicists, so that they can talk to you about lattice Q C D calculations of the decay properties of heavy mesons. *(Scanning the crowd)* The first speaker, post-doctoral fellow Henry Rainer.

(Polite applause. TROUSANT *looks for* HENRY *in the crowd.)*

TROUSANT: Henry? Henry? Henry!?

(A pause. No HENRY.*)*

TROUSANT: Son of a bitch.

*(*TROUSANT *storms away.* GINNY *follows* TROUSANT *like an energetic puppy. She doesn't see* CHRIS. *He sneaks up behind* GINNY.*)*

GINNY: Doctor Trousant—

TROUSANT: You did fine, Ginny—

GINNY: Hell, I did great. Look, I want to talk to you about this paper I'm working on—

TROUSANT: I am a very busy genius, you know. *(Looking down a hallway)* Henry!

*(*TROUSANT *storms ahead.* GINNY *follows.)*

GINNY: I read this piece in one of the theory journals—a thing about dark matter candidates, and I had some ideas about how to use the research that will come in from CRESST to—

TROUSANT: When I find him, I will do something very very violent.

GINNY: I was hoping to try to submit my work for the Haven Prize.

*(*TROUSANT *stops.)*

TROUSANT: You are an undergraduate. An undergraduate intern.

GINNY: Sure, but I'm right—

TROUSANT: Our department does not submit papers by undergraduates to compete for prestigious physics prizes.

GINNY: If you'd just read the darn thing—

(Interrupting them, CHRIS *swoops down, grabs* GINNY, *and spins her around.)*

CHRIS: Whoooo! Hey sugar!

GINNY: Chris! Oh my stars, Chris!

CHRIS: Hey baby doll, God I missed you.

GINNY: Chris! What are you doing here?

CHRIS: *(Kissing her)* Surprise.

TROUSANT: He does not look like a physicist.

GINNY: Sorry—Doctor Trousant, this is my fiancé, Chris.

TROUSANT: Perhaps, Ginny, you have more important things to do right now? I know I do.

GINNY: I'm sorry. No sir—it's just that he surprised me all the way from home—

TROUSANT: Henry! *(Uninterested, he marches off.)*

GINNY: Doctor Trousant?

CHRIS: I've got something for you.

GINNY: That man has no manners.

CHRIS: Don't you worry about it honey, you just step right over here.

*(*CHRIS *leads* GINNY *into her office. The* MINISTER *is waiting there.)*

GINNY: You know this is Illinois? Does your family know you've gone north of the Mason-Dixon line?

CHRIS: I came to rescue you.

GINNY: Lord knows I need it…I swear, I don't care if Doctor Trousant is God's gift to Science, it wouldn't kill him to— *(She sees the broken radio on her desk.)* What happened to my radio?

CHRIS: I've got a surprise.

GINNY: Looks like someone attacked it.

CHRIS: Your fiancé gets on a plane and comes all the way up here with a surprise and you're talking electronics.

(GINNY *notices the* MINISTER.)

GINNY: Who's he?

CHRIS: That's better.

MINISTER: Reverend John Hawkins.

GINNY: Who?

MINISTER: Many thanks. Your fiancé got me straight out of a deacon's meeting.

GINNY: You're a minister?

CHRIS: What do you say we get married, Ginny?

GINNY: I say it's a good idea. I just sent out the invitations.

CHRIS: What do you say we get married now?

GINNY: Now?

CHRIS: I can't wait three months. Let's go, just you, me, and the hijacked minister.

GINNY: Elope? Our parents would have a fit—

CHRIS: They've got eight hundred people coming to the wedding. Nobody can agree on a seating chart and already our parents are arguing about shrimp cocktail versus ham biscuits.

MINISTER: Eight hundred people?

GINNY: God, I get neck spasms just thinking about it.

CHRIS: See? Seems like weddings are always for everyone else. Let's have one just for us.

GINNY: Elope. It'd be scandalous…I'd love to be scandalous. People will think I'm pregnant.

CHRIS: Well, we can work on that too.

MINISTER: Maybe I should wait outside—

CHRIS: It's all right, stay.

GINNY: God, I'd love to just run off, but I can't. I'm here for three more months.

CHRIS: Well, I don't start work 'till after the honeymoon. I can stay, keep you company…I couldn't just leave my wife alone with all those little bitty specks.

GINNY: They're called leptons.

CHRIS: *(Rubbing her shoulders)* But do they rub your shoulders?

GINNY: Hardly.

CHRIS: Go on and pull one of those lepton pictures up on the computer.

GINNY: It's not a picture, it's more like a splat.

CHRIS: Whatever it is, if it's better than a back rub, I'll go home.

(GINNY *flips through images on her computer.*)

GINNY: Oh, it's mostly just splat. See, out there, the ring gets one proton racing around one way, then an anti-proton going the other way and then they smack into each other. It makes a big splat—like a fly on a car window.

MINISTER: Very romantic.

GINNY: Millions of collisions every second, most of them—boring. About one time in a billion you get something worth looking at.

CHRIS: You show me an explosion as exciting as you and me getting married.

GINNY: Like I said, one time in a billion.

CHRIS: So the odds against just picking one out are—

GINNY: Not nearly as good as the odds of me marrying you.

(*Playfully,* CHRIS *punches up an image on her screen—a circular graph with colored lines extending out to the edge like flower petals.*)

CHRIS: What do you think?

GINNY: Splat.

CHRIS: Exotic? Interesting? More wonderful than us?

(GINNY *smiles at him.*)

GINNY: Let's do it.

(*Gleefully,* CHRIS *picks her up and swings her into his arms.*)

(*Across the stage. Hallway under burnt-out light bulb.* FELIX *and* HENRY *enter.* FELIX *looks around expectantly.*)

FELIX: You think I'm crazy—

HENRY: I'm starting to get worried.

FELIX: I'm not crazy. I know. This is where you meet her. You see her for the first time right here. Between eight and nine o'clock.

HENRY: Eight and nine o'clock according to who?

FELIX: No, no, no—I am trying to set you up—don't talk to me about physics.

HENRY: I'm just saying—Einstein. Relativity. It's always eight according to someone. We could sit here forever.

FELIX: I talk about love and you talk about Einstein. You think this is good for your sex life?

HENRY: Not everybody gets a sex life. Some of us just get cool computers. *(He reaches into his bag and pulls out junk food.)*

FELIX: You believe me. Why else would you put up with me?

HENRY: What do you want, a candy bar?

FELIX: Snickers.

(HENRY gives FELIX a Snickers bar.)

HENRY: Destiny doesn't happen in hallways.

FELIX: Sure. Down the hall from the fire extinguisher, underneath the burned-out light bulb. Destiny has to happen somewhere.

(HENRY pours a cup of coffee from his Thermos. He checks his watch.)

HENRY: Almost nine.

(HENRY takes a flask out of his pocket and adds a shot of gin to the coffee. They wait in the silent hallway.)

FELIX: I guess maybe not today.

HENRY: I'm sorry, Felix.

FELIX: Not today. But someday. *(Dizzy, he sits down.)*

HENRY: Felix? You O K?

FELIX: Dizzy again. Maybe I've always been dizzy, right? Please, just sit here with me, the crazy janitor, right? We'll eat our snacks.

(HENRY sits. FELIX smiles.)

FELIX: Maybe she'll show up tomorrow.

(Outside the building. The MINISTER performs GINNY and CHRIS' marriage ceremony.)

MINISTER: For as much as Virginia and Christopher have consented together to holy wedlock, and have witnessed the same before God and before this company, I pronounce that they are Husband and Wife, in the name of the Father, the Son, and the Holy Spirit, Amen. What God has joined together, let not man put asunder... Congratulations. You may kiss the bride.

(CHRIS *and* GINNY *kiss.* GINNY *notices something in the distance.*)

CHRIS: (*Tipping the* MINISTER) Thank you very much.

(CHRIS *pulls* GINNY *close.*)

CHRIS: You ready for the honeymoon?

GINNY: Somebody's roller skating.

CHRIS: (*Kissing her neck*) Mmmmmmmmn.

GINNY: Across the way. There's a man teaching a woman how to roller skate. She looks like me. Don't you think she looks like me?

CHRIS: I don't know. I can't take my eyes off you.

GINNY: Marriage. Forever. You ready for this?

CHRIS: I have been ready my whole life.

(CHRIS *picks* GINNY *up and carries her away.*)

NOW + 1 DAY

(*Morning.* HENRY *works at his desk.* TROUSANT *enters.*)

TROUSANT: Henry!

(HENRY *chokes on his coffee.*)

HENRY: Doctor Trousant—you're angry, right? I figured you'd be really angry.

TROUSANT: I'm not going to yell. I yelled yesterday. Clearly, yelling is useless. I am however going to speak in a very firm tone.

HENRY: I hear that.

TROUSANT: Good. The Adler Planetarium High School Science Club.

HENRY: What?

TROUSANT: Hormone-crazed urchins who want to learn about science. You're giving a talk next month on the Heisenberg Uncertainty Principle.

HENRY: No, Doctor Trousant—really. I don't give talks. I don't talk. Speaking in general, I'm against it.

TROUSANT: I'm a generous sort of fellow, you know? Sure, after yesterday I ought to have you flogged, or hanged, or stripped naked and paraded through the proton beam. However, I have decided that you just need practice.

HENRY: Practice? This is deep psychological crap we're talking about here.

TROUSANT: I don't care what kind of genius you are, this lab needs scientists that—on occasion—actually speak to people. I've talked with the program advisory committee and they, of course, agree.

HENRY: You'd pull my funding? No, Armand. Look, how about flying? I'm not afraid of flying, you know. I'm completely macho about being thirty thousand feet in the air. Ask me to get on an airplane.

TROUSANT: You are not to miss one single presentation ever again—starting with the high school science club.

HENRY: I got wedgies in high school. Please.

TROUSANT: It's not that we like being tyrants. O K, we like it a little bit—but we're right, Henry. This lab was built by thousands of scientists working *together*. You may be brilliant, but what good are you if you're brilliant all by yourself?

(TROUSANT *leaves.* HENRY *follows him.*)

(*Across the stage.* GINNY *arrives for work.* FELIX *sweeps.*)

FELIX: Good morning, Ginny.

(GINNY *stops.*)

GINNY: I'm sorry, I don't remember. Have we met somewhere?

FELIX: Yesterday. Under the burnt-out light bulb. You met Henry and me? I was sort of the distinguished looking one—

GINNY: I don't think so—

FELIX: How's your blouse? Did you get the coffee out of your blouse? Cold water, soak it overnight right away—

GINNY: I'm sorry—coffee? I don't know what—

(*Suddenly dizzy,* FELIX *braces himself against her for balance.*)

GINNY: Are you all right?

(FELIX *tries to stand, but stumbles to the ground.* GINNY *swoops down to help him up.*)

GINNY: Sir? Sir!

(FELIX *looks up at her with a delighted smile.*)

FELIX: It's you.

(HENRY *enters. Seeing* FELIX, *he rushes over.*)

HENRY: Felix! Felix!

GINNY: Do you know this man?

HENRY: Felix, are you all right?

GINNY: He was by the door. He fell. I don't know—just bang—right over—

FELIX: (*To* HENRY) It's her—

HENRY: Who?

FELIX: From yesterday. Under the burned-out light bulb—

GINNY: I've never seen him before—

FELIX: You and her. Remember how you danced under the stars?

HENRY: What? No.

FELIX: You kissed her. There was a clarinet playing and you kissed her.

HENRY: Felix, you're confused. We've never met. *(To GINNY)* Have we?

GINNY: No.

FELIX: Yes. I remember.

GINNY: We should get him to a hospital.

FELIX: I'm fine. Really. You kids go on.

HENRY: You're not fine, you're babbling.

GINNY: *(To HENRY)* Ambulance or car?

HENRY: Ambulance.

(Sirens scream across the stage. Hospital. A curtain, medical equipment, and plastic chairs suggest a hospital room. FELIX lies asleep on a hospital bed. HENRY and GINNY sit by his side.)

HENRY: It's late. You should go.

GINNY: God, a brain tumor. I am so sorry—

HENRY: Your husband's probably worried—

GINNY: I called. He'll be all right.

HENRY: Look, no one sits at the hospital all day with a complete stranger.

GINNY: I do. You hungry? They have vending machines.

HENRY: I'm O K.

GINNY: Come on, I'll buy you some chips.

HENRY: Chips. No. Salt. Yuck.

GINNY: You don't like salt?

HENRY: It's not the taste—I don't mind the taste—it's the molecule.

GINNY: Sodium chloride.

HENRY: Yuck.

GINNY: You have something against sodium chloride.

HENRY: One sodium, one chlorine. Two little atoms, clinging together to make salt—like salt is so great and so profound—like they weren't better off just as plain old elements. But no—they think it's better to be salt— and they wander around causing high blood pressure and getting people hooked on snack foods and acting all high and mighty and chemically bonded until they get broken apart and there's nothing left but corrosive metal and toxic gas.

(GINNY *pulls a package of Fig Newtons and a carton of skim milk out of her bag.*)

GINNY: You got anything against sugar?

HENRY: You shouldn't try to help me.

GINNY: But you need help. You definitely need help. You hold grudges against molecules—you think that's normal?

HENRY: No.

(GINNY *eats her Fig Newtons.*)

GINNY: Henry Rainer. I've been wanting to meet you.

HENRY: Me?

GINNY: "Weakly Interacting Massive Particles and the Search for Dark Matter." I read your paper.

HENRY: You're an experimentalist. You're not even an experimentalist, you're an undergrad. What are you doing reading my papers?

GINNY: It's a hobby.

HENRY: Theoretical physics?

GINNY: Yeah. I mean, they go hand in hand, really. You predict something insane, we do the experiments that prove you wrong.

HENRY: You think I'm wrong?

GINNY: I think we could have a hell of a fight about it. And I think we could put that fight into the form of a paper *and* I think we could submit it for the Haven Prize. Dark Matter candidates: theory verses experiment.

HENRY: The Haven Prize. The lab's not going to submit an undergrad paper for the Haven Prize.

GINNY: That's why I need you.

HENRY: I don't write papers with other people.

GINNY: Rumor is, you don't do anything with other people.

HENRY: It's true.

(GINNY *notices a pair of roller skates next to* HENRY'*s bag.*)

GINNY: Were you roller skating?

HENRY: When?

GINNY: Yesterday, when I was getting married. I saw someone roller skating.

HENRY: Wasn't me.

GINNY: There was a girl roller skating and a guy holding her—that wasn't you?

HENRY: I was with Felix. We were sitting under a burnt-out light bulb all night waiting for destiny. She didn't show.

(FELIX *wakes up.*)

FELIX: Henry?

GINNY: You want me to stay with you?

HENRY: No. Go home.

GINNY: Look, I think you need—

HENRY: Go.

GINNY: All right then. We'll talk later.

(GINNY *packs up her things.* HENRY *sits next to* FELIX. *He holds* FELIX's *hand.*)

HENRY: I think I should be crying.

FELIX: I'm not dead yet.

HENRY: Most people would be crying.

FELIX: Someday, you'll cry. Sure. Someday. Not tonight.

HENRY: What are you going to do?

FELIX: Do? Light bulbs. I'm the only janitor that bothers changing the light bulbs. I have to get back to work.

HENRY: Do not go back to work.

FELIX: Three months to live. I've got to get busy. I should make up a diagram of the sockets, you know—for after I'm gone. It would be just like the rest of them to put one-twenty watt bulbs in the seventy-five watt sockets.

HENRY: Go to Hawaii or something, don't spend the last months of your life in Batavia, Illinois.

FELIX: I don't know anybody in Hawaii.

HENRY: But you want to work?

FELIX: It's what I do. It's what you do too. If it was you that was dying, you'd be staring at those numbers of yours to your last breath.

HENRY: Look, you could take a trip somewhere—

FELIX: No.

HENRY: There must be something you've always wanted to see.

(FELIX *peers around the curtain and sees* GINNY, *still on stage.*)

FELIX: It's her, Henry.

HENRY: Who? *(Following his gaze)* Her? I told her to go home.

FELIX: Remember? Last night. Under the light bulb. BAM—Destiny.

HENRY: Felix, she wasn't there. I never saw her in my life before today.

FELIX: Yesterday. She was upset. She bumped into you, spilled coffee all over your shirt—remember? You were drinking coffee.

HENRY: She got married yesterday—eloped. She told me.

FELIX: She wants you to work on something together—a paper.

HENRY: How'd you know that?

FELIX: I told you—we met her. You said yes to the paper? You should say yes.

HENRY: Felix, the doctors say you're going to be getting confused—

FELIX: Yes, yes. I'm confused. I'm crazy. I've got a big tumor squeezing wacky thoughts out of my head. But what do you science people say—it's all relative?

HENRY: We say there is no way of picking one frame of reference over another...then there's some math.

FELIX: So, we're both right. It just depends on where you stand.

HENRY: Yes, well I'm standing over here with the people who have a grip on reality.

FELIX: You should come to my side. It's much more interesting.

NOW + 4 DAYS

(Outside HENRY's apartment. GINNY looks for his apartment number. HENRY exits with a bag of laundry, some books, and a large poster board.)

HENRY: Ginny. What are you doing outside my apartment?

GINNY: You weren't at work. I was worried.

HENRY: You were worried. About me?

GINNY: Worried. And I wanted to talk to you about this paper—

HENRY: You know, I'm busy. I'm crazed. I've got Felix dying, and laundry to do, and now Doctor Trousant's got me spending the next month working up a lecture for a high school science club.

GINNY: It might help you, you know. Working with someone? It might take your mind off things.

HENRY: *(Pointing to his poster)* I am working with someone. It's me and Heisenberg.

(HENRY shows GINNY his poster. It's filled with complicated equations.)

GINNY: You're showing that poster to kids?

HENRY: Yeah. What?

GINNY: Quantum field equations?

HENRY: They take math.

GINNY: High school. They take algebra.

(HENRY looks at his poster—finally seeing it through the eyes of a teenager and not a grad student.)

HENRY: Oh God!

GINNY: Don't get into the math. Forget the math. Just talk to them.

HENRY: Yeah, well there's a little problem with that. I suppose you know about glossophobia—

GINNY: Try being a person. Plain English. The Heisenberg Uncertainty Principle.

HENRY: Right. The electron has a probability wave associated with—

GINNY: They aren't physicists, Henry. You just tell them, electrons are weird—

HENRY: Weird.

GINNY: Like a teacher. You know how, in grade school, there was always one teacher who seemed to be everywhere? For me—Mrs Standon—second grade— It's like that.

HENRY: Who?

GINNY: You'd be chewing gum, and you'd see Mrs Standon in the hallway—big trouble, right? So you'd duck around the corner and bam—there she was, suddenly in the music room. Weird. An electron is like that—it exists everywhere when you're not looking, but you only see it one place at a time.

HENRY: See, that's great! It's you. You're friendly and you're perky, and you make sense, and I'm...me.

GINNY: You'll be fine.

HENRY: I'll get bogged down, start muttering about radioactive decay and they'll eat me alive. (*He paces.*)

GINNY: Sit down, you're making me nervous.

HENRY: Look, thanks for the advice, but—

GINNY: How about a trade?

HENRY: A trade.

GINNY: I need help with this paper for the Haven Prize.
You need help with your presentation.

HENRY: We work together.

GINNY: Yes.

HENRY: I don't do that.

GINNY: But you're desperate.

HENRY: I'm always desperate.

GINNY: But this time you have help.

(HENRY *sits.*)

HENRY: Look, I should tell you something about
Felix—

GINNY: Felix?

HENRY: You should know…he thinks we're destined
for each other—

(GINNY *bursts out laughing.*)

GINNY: That's great! Priceless!

HENRY: It's not great.

GINNY: You think it will make me uncomfortable?

HENRY: Doesn't it?

GINNY: I am very happily married.

HENRY: It makes me uncomfortable.

GINNY: O K, do the presentation alone. Lose your
funding. You'll be the only fry guy at McDonald's with
a PhD in theoretical physics.

HENRY: You heard about my funding?

GINNY: Word is, you're just about a lost cause. I love a
lost cause.

HENRY: Felix is coming back to work, you know. He's coming back and he's got this whole story about how you bumped into me under a burnt-out light bulb and spilled coffee—he thinks it's destiny.

GINNY: Are there any coffee stains on your clothes? In your laundry?

HENRY: No.

GINNY: Trust me, I'm harmless.

HENRY: I'm acting crazy right? It's crazy. Felix has some hallucination about how we met two days ago and I flip out. Forget it. I'll do the paper. I'm fine.

(CHRIS *enters with car keys.*)

CHRIS: *(To* GINNY*)* You ready, honey? I can park.

GINNY: Don't bother, I'll just be a second.

(CHRIS *ducks out.* GINNY *turns to leave—then stops.*)

GINNY: He knew my name.

HENRY: Huh?

GINNY: Felix. Yesterday. I was walking in the building. He was sweeping up. He looked right at me and said "Good morning, Ginny." I'd never seen him before in my life and he knew my name.

HENRY: Well, that could be….

GINNY: From the nameplate on my cubicle.

HENRY: Or a phone list.

GINNY: I'm sure it's nothing.

HENRY: Nothing.

(GINNY *leaves.*)

NOW + 1 WEEK

(A cafeteria table. GINNY *sits with* CHRIS. *They hold hands like high school sweethearts.)*

GINNY: So Taylor said the whole town's in an uproar. Mrs Hampton from the bridal shop called my parents' house in tears, wondering if my dress should still be white, because they just didn't have time to order it in champagne or ivory. Well, my mother said of course it would be white, and just what exactly was she suggesting? I'm telling you—a battle, with *Emily Post's Book of Etiquette* caught right in the crossfire—

*(*HENRY *enters. Ignoring* CHRIS, HENRY *takes a seat next to* GINNY.*)*

HENRY: I have a real problem with Switzerland.

GINNY: Switzerland?

HENRY: Switzerland. Small country. Right between Germany and—

GINNY: I know where Switzerland is.

HENRY: Well I have a problem with it.

CHRIS: Excuse me, we were having lunch.

HENRY: I agreed to do your paper, but I didn't think that we might have to present it—

GINNY: It's the Haven prize; the finalists present in Switzerland.

HENRY: I don't present papers. Not here. Definitely not in Europe. Definitely not all the way around the world in a room filled with hundreds of scientists.

GINNY: Look, the lab can only send one paper a year to compete for the Haven Prize and Doctor Trousant hates me. I don't think we'll get picked.

HENRY: But what if we do?

GINNY: Then you go to Switzerland.

HENRY: Oh no. You go to Switzerland.

CHRIS: What's he talking about, honey?

GINNY: *(To* CHRIS*)* I'm not going anywhere.

HENRY: Oh yes you are—I am not flying across the ocean, then getting up there in front of hundreds— *hundreds*—of people—

GINNY: You'll do fine—

CHRIS: You have to present a paper?

HENRY: Who's he?

GINNY: Henry, this is my husband. I have a husband. This is Chris.

CHRIS: It's a pleasure.

HENRY: Tell her to go to Switzerland.

CHRIS: I could exchange the honeymoon tickets. We could go.

GINNY: I'd rather be in Hawaii.

HENRY: The thing is—I'm a little desperate—I can't talk in front of people. Usually I can't even talk to people. I get nauseous and nervous and I hide under furniture.

GINNY: You hide under furniture.

HENRY: I told you—I'm no good at presentations.

GINNY: But you hide?

HENRY: Yes. So you can see, that the thought of having to go to Switzerland—

GINNY: Look, you're helping me, right?

HENRY: Yes.

GINNY: So, I'll help you.

HENRY: You think you can do that?

GINNY: Henry, by the time I'm done with you, you'll be saying things you never thought possible.

HENRY: Sounds terrifying. Look, please. If you won't do it for me, do it for your PhD.

GINNY: I'm not getting a PhD.

HENRY: Sure you are.

GINNY: I'm married. I'm graduating. I'm done.

HENRY: You're a physics major. You have an internship at Fermilab.

GINNY: I have life. This is just killing time 'till I can get back to civilization.

CHRIS: To Ginny, that means South Carolina.

HENRY: But what about Switzerland?

GINNY: You read the paper. I'll be on a beach, with my husband, without a scientist in sight.

HENRY: You don't turn down a symposium on quantum cosmology, that's nuts.

GINNY: Henry, I am the only one here who's perfectly sane.

(GINNY and CHRIS leave together.)

NOW + 2 WEEKS

(GINNY's office. Books and papers spill across the table. GINNY and HENRY work. They have been at this for hours.)

HENRY: Here, look at this. It's Trousant's paper.

GINNY: Trousant.

HENRY: Look, he uses the renormalization group equations here. You should ask him about it.

GINNY: I'd feel strange. He scares me.

HENRY: Doctor Trousant? He's all right. Deep down. Way deep down.

GINNY: He scares me. And that German guy. The one who grunts—

HENRY: Now, he's terrifying—

GINNY: They all scare me. Everyone here. I mean I try, I try to get along but—like the German guy, I gave him a hug today and I thought he was going to collapse—

HENRY: You gave him a hug?

GINNY: He found a journal I was looking for—I just got so excited—

HENRY: You hugged the German plasma physics guy?

GINNY: His name is Hans.

HENRY: You hugged Hans?

GINNY: I was excited. And I thought maybe he needed one. He never smiles, have you noticed that?

HENRY: *(Laughing)* Yes.

GINNY: See, you're laughing. You think it's silly. I thought I was just being nice.

HENRY: You are nice.

GINNY: I don't really fit in here, do I?

HENRY: Nobody fits in here.

GINNY: I'm just not like you people. Intense. Working all the time. If I were home, you know what I'd be doing on a night like this? I'd be sitting out under the stars.

HENRY: You are under the stars.

GINNY: They look like fluorescent lights.

(HENRY points to various papers pinned to the wall: a physics poster, scraps of notes, etc.)

HENRY: Here. Einstein's laws govern the fusion of stars. Kepler, the orbits of the planets. Hubble calculated the expansion of the universe, Maxwell—

GINNY: The equations for light.

HENRY: You're right here in your office and it's the best view in the galaxy.

GINNY: You know Henry, you are not what you seem.

HENRY: Neither are you. Talk to Trousant. You'll do fine.

GINNY: All right. I'll ask him about the paper. But no hugs.

HENRY: Deal. *(He returns to his books.)*

GINNY: No. No work. Not right now. Let's just sit for a while.

(They admire the view of the papers on the wall. GINNY eats her Fig Newtons. HENRY takes out a Thermos of coffee and a flask.)

GINNY: You hungry?

HENRY: I'm thirsty.

GINNY: What's that? Coffee and…

HENRY: Gin.

GINNY: In your coffee?

HENRY: Trust me. Quantum theory makes a lot more sense.

(FELIX enters with a janitor's cart. He whistles a romantic love ballad as he cleans the office.)

HENRY: *(Whispering to GINNY)* You don't think he'll get any ideas do you? Because we're here late?

GINNY: What ideas?

HENRY: Ideas about you and me.

FELIX: I already have plenty of ideas.

HENRY: I'm here because of the work.

GINNY: I know.

HENRY: I just don't want anybody to get any ideas.

GINNY: You afraid I might kiss you?

HENRY: Ginny!

GINNY: I'm kidding. Just relax. It's nothing—

(FELIX empties the trash. He notices something sparkle. He picks it up—an engagement ring. He gives it to GINNY.)

FELIX: Is this your ring?

GINNY: Oh my God, how'd I lose— *(She looks at her finger. Her ring is still there.)*

HENRY: Wow, they look alike.

GINNY: All engagement rings look alike.

HENRY: They look exactly alike.

GINNY: Somebody must have lost it.

HENRY: In your trash can.

GINNY: You'd better take this, Felix.

FELIX: It's not mine.

GINNY: I can't keep it.

FELIX: We'll put up a sign.

GINNY: Poor thing she must be frantic. *(Spooked, she puts the ring in her desk.)*

HENRY: Ginny?

GINNY: I guess we should get back to work.

HENRY: No. No physics. Come on, I'll help you make some signs.

GINNY: Please.

NOW + 8 WEEKS

(HENRY's office. HENRY hides.)

GINNY: (O S) Henry!? Hennnry?! Henry?

(GINNY enters. She finds HENRY.)

HENRY: Ginny. I'm hiding.

GINNY: (Gently) Henry, the Adler Planetarium High School Science Club? Doctor Trousant is waiting.

HENRY: Yeah, that—I don't think I can go.

GINNY: We had a deal.

HENRY: I helped you with the paper—

GINNY: And I help you with this.

HENRY: Look, I was just reading our paper. It's good work.

GINNY: Really? Good?

HENRY: Excellent, Ginny. It's going to get chosen, you know. It's going to get chosen and they're going to want us to present it to all those scientists in Switzerland—I can't even get up the nerve to talk to a bunch of kids down the hall.

GINNY: You have to do this.

HENRY: Trousant can just fire me.

GINNY: You have to do this for me.

HENRY: You don't need my help anymore.

GINNY: (Looking at the paper) It's excellent? In another month I'll be back home. I'll start a job teaching trigonometry at the same school that once taught me to count to twenty. I'll have all my family and my best friends. I'll have Chris. I'll have everything I've ever wanted, but I won't have this. And that's all right. It's all right because I did something excellent. You have to present this paper, Henry. In Switzerland or on street corners or anywhere that anybody will listen.

HENRY: It's not that I want to let you down. I don't want to let you down.

GINNY: I need you to be able to talk to people. Please. I need you to learn to do it for me.

HENRY: All right. I might faint or throw up, but all right.

(HENRY *takes* GINNY'S *hand.*)

(*Podium.* GINNY *and* HENRY *present to the high school science club.* GINNY *is poised, graceful, and confident. A nervous* HENRY *stands next to her. He does his best to blend into the floor.* FELIX *and* TROUSANT *watch from the back.* GINNY *turns on an overhead projector. The white light shoots onto the screen.*)

GINNY: If an electron exists everywhere when we're not looking, but only shows up one place at a time, the question is: How does it know which way to be?

(GINNY *steps back in order to give* HENRY *the floor. He doesn't take it. He stands frozen like a deer in the headlights.*)

GINNY: Henry?

HENRY: If an electron exists everywhere when we're not looking, but only shows up—

(GINNY *stops him.*)

GINNY: (*Whispering*) I just said that.

(*Frantic,* HENRY *flips through his notes.*)

HENRY: So—the electron—it's either like in a kind of— well, um…the Heisenberg Uncertainty Principle…in quantum mechanics—it's kind of like… The electron—

(GINNY *steps in to rescue him.*)

GINNY: Electrons are weird. Like maybe my friend Henry here.

HENRY: Me?

GINNY: Henry is hard to size up. Sometimes he can be one thing, sometimes he can be another—it depends on how you look at him.

HENRY: I should sit down.

GINNY: Henry, you are a visual aid, you stay here. *(To the students)* The point is, you never know which way it's going to go. Neither does he. Yet. It turns out that, according to physics, there's no reason that certain types of waves can't travel both forward and backward in time.

(GINNY uses an overhead projector to project her diagrams onto the screen.)

HENRY: Right, both ways—

(GINNY draws an X on the screen.)

GINNY: *(To HENRY)* See, you're doing fine. *(To the class)* So our guy is standing here, and he's sending out waves into the future and into the past.

(GINNY draws a wave going forward from the X.)

GINNY: "What am I? What am I?" he says. "Am I a neurotic electron, in desperate need of therapy, way out in la la land, personal issues smeared out all over the place and no clue about where I am or where I'm going? Or am I a ground state electron—calm, relaxed, hanging out near the nucleus with his psychological act together?"

HENRY: I don't know—

GINNY: That's right, you don't know—yet. But these waves travel out around him, until somewhere out here— *(To the right of the first X, she draws another X on the screen.)* Somewhere out here in the future, it meets

another electron. This electron hears the question,
"What am I? Hopelessly lost? Or at home with my
feet on the ground?" So, the electron takes a look.
(To HENRY*)* It looks at him and it says, "Well, you're
standing here aren't you? I think there's hope for you
yet."

HENRY: *(To the students)* You should know that there's
no way to prove any of this. It's just a theory.

(GINNY *draws a wave going backward from the second X. It
meets the wave from the first X and cancels it out.)*

GINNY: And this interaction sends out another set of
waves in both directions in time. The two waves cancel
each other out everywhere in the universe except
(Pointing at the first X) between this moment *(Pointing at
the second X)* and this moment.

HENRY: So it's not just the past that changes the future,
it's the future that changes the past.

GINNY: Like shaking hands, making sure that
everything stays together.

HENRY: Yes.

(Applause)

(Later, in HENRY's *office:* FELIX *and* HENRY *drink.)*

FELIX: You are calming down. Good. This sweaty panic
thing—it is not attractive.

(HENRY *gulps down his drink.)*

HENRY: Nerves.

FELIX: She's pretty, yes?

HENRY: Quantum non-locality, Heisenberg. Oh my
God, did you hear her talking tonight? I guess I just
have this thing for a beautiful woman explaining
quantum physics.

FELIX: You should tell her that.

HENRY: No. You know what this is?

FELIX: Love?

HENRY: Hormones. Specifically testosterone. Getting pumped through my body because I was nervous—perfectly natural. It will go away.

FELIX: Who wants it to go away?

(GINNY *enters.*)

FELIX: Time for me to leave you two alone.

HENRY: No, no—Felix—it's—

(Too late. FELIX *has left.)*

GINNY: You were great tonight!

HENRY: I was a disaster.

GINNY: A little nervous—

HENRY: I couldn't speak.

GINNY: You didn't spend the evening in a closet. I count that as a triumph.

HENRY: At least Doctor Trousant was happy.

GINNY: Just wait 'till they hear you in Switzerland.

HENRY: You're crazy.

GINNY: Yes, and it's fabulous. Why not Switzerland? Do you know that I can do anything? I have delusions of grandeur. Me! I mean, I'm twenty-two years old and I just finished a paper trying to explain missing mass in the universe. The universe is a very big place, Henry.

HENRY: I've heard that.

GINNY: It's a very big place, and thanks to you, I've got a piece of it.

(GINNY *smiles at* HENRY. *The kind of smile that melts men's hearts.* CHRIS *enters.)*

CHRIS: Ginny, you told me nine o'clock. It's ten fifteen.

GINNY: Sorry about the time, sweetie. Henry and I got caught up with everything.

CHRIS: Ah.

HENRY: But we've finished the paper.

GINNY: We're celebrating. Come on. Stay. Have a beer. You two should—I don't know—be friends.

(GINNY *thrusts a drink in his hands. She leaves to pack her bag.* CHRIS *sits down next to* HENRY—*sizing him up. A long awkward pause.*)

CHRIS: Celebrating. So, you're all done.

HENRY: It's a great paper.

CHRIS: Then maybe Ginny and I can head home.

HENRY: South Carolina?

CHRIS: Sure.

HENRY: She's supposed to be here for another three weeks.

CHRIS: But you're done.

HENRY: She still has the internship.

CHRIS: Come on, you guys are a bunch of highfalutin' scientists. What do you need Ginny for?

HENRY: She's a scientist.

CHRIS: Yeah, she's always been real good at math.

HENRY: Real good. She writes about experiments with cryogenic subatomic particle detectors.

CHRIS: Physics, calculus, it's all easy for her. Hell, even bonus points. You know those credit card award programs? Ginny keeps them all in her head. In school, she used to call, all excited, saying she'd saved enough reward points for us to get a hotel room.

HENRY: That's adorable.

CHRIS: That's my Ginny. You know, we should be friends, really. I mean, you're friends with Ginny. I'm married to Ginny—we should—I don't know—do you play golf?

HENRY: Not at all.

(*Awkward silence.* GINNY *returns.*)

GINNY: You two getting acquainted?

HENRY: Your husband wants to go home.

GINNY: What?

CHRIS: It's nothing.

HENRY: He was just saying to me—

CHRIS: I was saying—well, you are done, right?

GINNY: Just with the paper. I still have a few weeks.

HENRY: You could go back without her.

CHRIS: I don't know if—

GINNY: No, I don't do much without Chris, never have.

CHRIS: We're a team. Ginny and me. She stays, I stay. And when I go, she goes.

GINNY: You see, Henry?

HENRY: I see.

(CHRIS *wraps his arms around* GINNY.)

NOW + 9 WEEKS

(*Late.* GINNY *works under the stars.* HENRY *and* TROUSANT *enter.*)

HENRY: It's us.

GINNY: What?

TROUSANT: It's your paper.

HENRY: You're brilliant. I'm brilliant. You and I are so fucking brilliant!

(HENRY *picks* GINNY *up and spins her around.*)

TROUSANT: Congratulations, Ginny, you are the youngest person ever to be sent by this lab to compete for the Haven Prize.

GINNY: It's us? I didn't actually think we'd get picked—

HENRY: Pack your bags, we're going to Switzerland!

GINNY: Switzerland? I'm not going to Switzerland.

HENRY: You're going.

GINNY: Henry, we talked about this.

HENRY: That was before we won.

GINNY: No, Henry. Doctor Trousant, Henry will have to present the paper without me.

HENRY: I can't do that.

GINNY: Henry, get over it. All you have to do is stand up there and read the darn thing. Just picture them all in their underwear or something.

HENRY: This isn't about me, this is about you. You are going to Switzerland, you are going to stand up in front of those people, and it is going to launch your career into the stratosphere—and do you know why? Because you will be the youngest person ever to present at this conference, and the only woman, and most of all, because you deserve it.

GINNY: There is no career. I am not going to graduate school. I want to go home—back home, where I belong.

TROUSANT: We thought, perhaps, that this opportunity would change your mind.

GINNY: Thank you, Doctor Trousant. No.

TROUSANT: All right then. You don't go.

HENRY: Doctor Trousant—

TROUSANT: We do not kidnap people and force them to graduate school, Henry. You heard her. She is not going. We don't want scientists who don't want us. *(He leaves.)*

HENRY: You are not going to Switzerland.

GINNY: You're upset.

HENRY: I thought I knew you, Ginny. I thought you understood what was important

GINNY: Physics.

HENRY: You majored in it, didn't you?

GINNY: You have to major in something.

HENRY: You've got insight that people work their whole lives for.

GINNY: I do understand what's important, Henry. I've got a whole life waiting for me. Why don't you think that's enough?

HENRY: *(Waving the paper)* I don't know. A hunch.

GINNY: Great.

(HENRY pulls a pair of roller skates out of his bag.)

HENRY: You want to go roller skating?

GINNY: No.

HENRY: I think it will help.

GINNY: Just let's stand—stand still and figure this out.

HENRY: Just have to have your feet on the ground.

GINNY: The ground is a very good place for feet.

HENRY: It's boring. Has no vision.

GINNY: Not like roller skating.

HENRY: Sure. Relativity. Einstein. Move fast enough and the rest of the universe slows down for you to take a look at it.

GINNY: You're going ten miles an hour.

HENRY: O K, so it doesn't slow down by much.

GINNY: Less than a quadrillionth of each second.

HENRY: Sometimes, that's all you need.

GINNY: What exactly do you do, Henry?

HENRY: Do?

GINNY: Up there in your office all day—Really, I want to know. The rest of us are down in the lab working with five thousand tons of electronics and computers and radioactive material and you're up on the third floor—what—thinking?

HENRY: Sometimes, I doodle.

GINNY: I've seen your work. Weakly Interactive Massive Particles? I mean as long as you don't have to prove anything, lord—go nuts. Why not write an equation that says the universe sits on the belly of a basset hound?

HENRY: It happens to be a ten-dimensional basset hound.

GINNY: I see.

HENRY: Look, we have something between us, don't we? I mean, I feel something there. A certain energy, honesty, whatever—

GINNY: Whatever.

HENRY: So I can tell you...you're a liar. This whole sweet southern "just give me a bridge club and a mint julep" thing is a lie. Simple-minded socialites do not get college internships at Fermilab. They do not stay

up late doing extra research on international particle
physics experiments.

GINNY: It was just some thoughts.

HENRY: Not thoughts, vision.

GINNY: Henry, I have a plan—I've had a plan since
I was six years old. I love my life. I just can't throw
everything to the wind. I want things that are certain,
like—like—

HENRY: Like Chris.

(GINNY *doesn't answer.*)

HENRY: Does he know how brilliant you are?

GINNY: I wish you wouldn't act like it's so all fired
important.

HENRY: He doesn't know.

GINNY: The important thing is, he doesn't care!

HENRY: I see.

(GINNY *gets up to leave.*)

HENRY: You can't leave you know. Underneath this
ring, particles can move close to the speed of light.
Einstein. Relativity. The rest of the universe slows
down for them to take a look. From this place, it'll take
you two years just to reach the parking lot.

(HENRY *leaves.* GINNY *stands—trapped.*)

NOW + 10 WEEKS

(GINNY *hasn't moved.* CHRIS *enters.*)

CHRIS: Ginny, there you are.

GINNY: Chris, what are you doing here? It's past
midnight.

CHRIS: I've been looking everywhere. I thought maybe you were with Henry.

GINNY: He left.

CHRIS: Funny, isn't it? You weren't in your office, so the first place I think to go look for my wife is with him.

GINNY: He left a while ago.

CHRIS: I mean, that's the first place I look.

GINNY: He left two years ago.

CHRIS: Seems like you're always with Henry.

GINNY: Not right now.

CHRIS: Ginny, I don't want you spending any more time with him.

GINNY: What?

CHRIS: I just don't think it's a good idea.

GINNY: We're working together.

CHRIS: Not anymore. You're done. Just don't see him any more—please.

GINNY: Chris, honey, you're being ridiculous.

CHRIS: I am?

GINNY: Yes.

(CHRIS laughs with relief.)

CHRIS: I am. Good. Thank God. I thought it was ridiculous.

GINNY: Well of course it is. After all we've been through together, you're worried about me and Henry and two more weeks?

CHRIS: I'm crazy O K? I imagine all sorts of possibilities that have nothing to do with the truth.

GINNY: Did Felix say something to you?

CHRIS: Who?

GINNY: Felix. The janitor.

CHRIS: What would he say?

GINNY: He's got this whole thing about me and Henry and destiny.

CHRIS: A thing.

GINNY: It's nothing. He gets confused.

CHRIS: You're sure?

GINNY: He has a brain tumor. He gets confused.

CHRIS: But we've got it straight, right? We know what we want?

GINNY: We do.

NOW + 12 WEEKS

(*At the hospital.* GINNY *sits by* FELIX's *side. His face is gray with cancer.* HENRY *enters.*)

GINNY: He can't see.

HENRY: Felix?

GINNY: He was fine this morning—we were talking—and then nothing. The doctors, they don't think...

HENRY: Felix, can you hear me?

FELIX: I'm blind, not deaf.

(HENRY *takes* FELIX's *hand.* GINNY *packs up her things.*)

GINNY: I'm glad you're here now. He needs you here. I mean, I'm going home soon and in a few weeks you'll be on your way to Europe.

HENRY: Without you.

(FELIX *smiles and does a little dance in his chair.*)

GINNY: You're pretty good.

FELIX: I am a championship dancer. Like you.

GINNY: No, not me.

FELIX: You and Henry—dancing out there under the stars?

GINNY: Henry dances?

FELIX: He dances with you.

HENRY: No, Felix.

FELIX: Yes. I saw. I say so.

GINNY: I didn't dance with him, Felix.

FELIX: Don't worry. It's our secret. We won't tell your husband. He might get upset.

HENRY: Felix, you get confused, remember?

FELIX: There was no dancing?

GINNY: No. And it's very important you don't say something like that.

FELIX: No dancing.

HENRY: No dancing. Just a little fighting.

GINNY: But it's all right.

(*A tear runs down* FELIX's *cheek.*)

GINNY: Oh, Felix.

FELIX: I'm sorry.

GINNY: Don't cry.

FELIX: Yes. Why should I cry? I know.

(CHRIS *enters.*)

CHRIS: Ginny? You ready?

GINNY: All right, then. We'll leave you two alone.

(GINNY *kisses* FELIX's *cheek.* CHRIS *leaves. As* GINNY *passes* HENRY, *he pulls her into a deep hug.*)

HENRY: You're going to be all right.

GINNY: No, I'm not.

(GINNY *lets him go. She walks out.*)

HENRY: You were right about her.

FELIX: Yes I was.

(HENRY *looks at his friend, lying on the edge of death's door. He takes* FELIX's *hand.*)

HENRY: Felix, I just want you to know how much our friendship has meant—I don't know what I'm going to do—

FELIX: Wait. Hold on. Stop. This is good. Good stuff. Don't waste it on me. I'm dying.

HENRY: It's not a waste—

FELIX: You love me, you can't bear to see me go. You should save this for her.

HENRY: Ginny.

FELIX: Tears in your eyes. Heart on your sleeve. Women love this stuff.

HENRY: She's leaving Friday with her husband. They're starting their life together.

FELIX: I have a secret for you. The really big decisions in life aren't the ones that change the future. Changing the future is easy. The big ones come when we change the past. Tell her you love her—tell her and it will make every moment you've ever had together... blossom.

HENRY: Oh, right—Ginny, even though you are married to a fabulously handsome, rich, successful guy who you adore, it's not a big deal. The important thing, of course, is that I'm in love with you—

FELIX: Yes. Like that. Good.

HENRY: It wouldn't change her mind.

FELIX: The important thing is it would change you. Tell her how you danced with her under the stars and how you kissed her while the clarinet music was playing.

HENRY: I never did that. I don't do that. I'm a scientist—a geek since I was four years old. I don't blossom. I don't explode into passion. I get nauseous and sweaty and I mutter.

FELIX: You did do it. Somewhere, some part of you did. I know. I remember.

NOW + 13 WEEKS

(FELIX's *funeral. The* RABBI *closes the service with a prayer.* CHRIS *drapes a protective arm around* GINNY's *shoulder.* HENRY *stands numbly.*)

RABBI: *Eil malei rachamim sho-khein bam'romim, hamm-tzei m'nukhah n'khonah tahat kanfei ha-sh'khinah, b'ma-alot k'doshim u-t'horimk'zohar ha-rakiya maz-hirim et nishmat Felix ben Chaim she-halakh l'olamo, b'gan eiden t'hei m'nuhato. Ana, ba-al ha-rahamim, hassti-rei-hu b'seiter k'nafekha l'olamim, u-tzror bi-tzror ha-hayim et nishmato, Adonai hu nahalato, v'yanu-ah b'shalom al mishkavo v'nomar amen.*

(*Translation: God of compassion, grant perfect peace in your sheltering presence, among the holy and the pure who shine in the brightness of the firmament, to the soul of our dear Felix Rosenbaum who has gone to his eternal rest. God of compassion, remember all his worthy deeds in the land of the living. May his soul be bound up in the bond of everlasting life. May God be his inheritance. May he rest in peace. And let us answer: Amen.*)

(GINNY *leaves* CHRIS *and joins* HENRY *by the grave.*)

GINNY: He adored you, you know.

HENRY: I know.

(GINNY *gives* HENRY *the engagement ring that* FELIX *found.*)

GINNY: Henry, I was wondering if you'd hold on to this for me?

HENRY: The engagement ring.

GINNY: Nobody ever claimed it. I just feel awful, you know. Whoever she is, she's probably frantic. You'll look for her?

HENRY: I'll look for her.

(*Suddenly nervous,* HENRY *takes* GINNY'*s hand.*)

HENRY: Look, Ginny I promised Felix I'd do something—say something to you—I'm just—I don't think—

GINNY: I don't believe in destiny.

HENRY: Yeah.

GINNY: I believe in choices. I have made choices. Permanent, irrevocable, decisions about my life.

HENRY: So, I guess this is it, then.

GINNY: We have a six o'clock flight.

HENRY: Good-bye, Ginny.

(*Tears in her eyes,* GINNY *hugs him.*)

GINNY: Good-bye, Henry. Take care.

(GINNY *leaves with* CHRIS.)

(*Airport. Sounds of a crowded terminal. A voice on the loudspeaker.* GINNY *and* CHRIS *walk through with their bags. A* MUSICIAN *with a clarinet puts out his hat.*)

VOICE: May I have your attention please. We are ready to begin boarding for flight one thirty-seven, service to Greenville. First class and premiere mileage passengers may now board at this time.

GINNY: Chris? Do you believe in destiny?

CHRIS: Sure.

GINNY: You do?

CHRIS: How do you suppose that out of all the towns in all the world, you and I were born and raised just a few blocks away from each other?

GINNY: That's not destiny, that's probability. Statistically speaking, the odds are good that two people—like us—who grew up together would naturally become attached—

CHRIS: Attached—

GINNY: I am with you because of experimental data.

CHRIS: We're not attached—we're married.

GINNY: Data. I have been collecting data. Twenty-two years plus three months and six days worth of data. That's how long we've known each other. With five leap years, it's one thousand one hundred sixty-one weeks and four days.

CHRIS: We've known each other forever.

GINNY: Eight thousand one hundred and thirty-one days. One hundred ninety-five thousand one hundred and fifty *(She looks at the clock.)* fifty-two hours.

CHRIS: Math. Ginny, we're going home and you're doing math.

GINNY: I'm just saying that I have a lot of experimental evidence to suggest that you are absolutely positively the man I am supposed to be with for the rest of my life.

CHRIS: Honey, are you all right?

GINNY: I'm better than all right, I'm scientifically validated.

CHRIS: Good. Just as long as you're happy.

GINNY: Perfectly happy. Ecstatic. I have eleven million, seven hundred nine thousand, one hundred and about twenty minutes that say everything right now is absolutely perfect.

CHRIS: Perfect.

VOICE: Continuing the boarding call for flight one thirty-seven, passengers seated in rows fifteen through thirty, fifteen through thirty may now board at this time.

GINNY: There's a snack stand. I'll be right back.

CHRIS: We're boarding.

GINNY: They have Fig Newtons. I'll be right back.

CHRIS: I'll take care of it. *(He leaves.)*

(The MUSICIAN *begins to play the clarinet. The music echoes through the room. Time stops.* GINNY *stops.* HENRY *roller skates across the stage. He sweeps* GINNY *into a kiss. Wrapped in his embrace,* GINNY *kisses him back. Until she remembers…)*

GINNY: Henry. What are you—Henry, I can't—I'm married.

HENRY: No you're not.

GINNY: I am. I'm— *(She looks down at her hand. Her wedding ring is gone.)*

GINNY: Where's my ring?

HENRY: I was standing in the hallway—underneath a burnt-out light bulb—

GINNY: Please—

HENRY: You came running down the hall, you were upset. You ran into me—spilled coffee all over my shirt—

GINNY: You're talking like Felix.

HENRY: We talked all night after that. I fell in love with you.

GINNY: Henry, if I could—

HENRY: Remember the time we danced under the stars?

(HENRY *hears the clarinet music.*)

HENRY: Listen. Remember—remember Felix? He said I kissed you while the clarinet music played. You remember.

(GINNY *kisses* HENRY.)

HENRY: I have been looking for you, Ginny. That's what we do, isn't it? We look. There are millions of collisions a second, billions a day, and we look hoping to find the one that's unique, exotic. And it does happen, we exhaust every possibility and we find the ones that give us a glimpse into the nature of the universe.

GINNY: I can't just change things, Henry. My life is with Chris, I can't just change that. Not now.

(HENRY *kisses her.*)

HENRY: No. Not now.

(GINNY *pulls herself from* HENRY *and walks away.*)

HENRY: It's all right, Ginny. We have a whole future together. You just don't remember it yet.

(HENRY *watches* GINNY *leave with her husband.*)

END OF ACT ONE

ACT TWO

NOW + 13 WEEKS

(FELIX's *funeral. The* RABBI *closes the service with a prayer.* CHRIS *drapes a protective arm around* GINNY's *shoulder.* HENRY *stands over the coffin. He is smiling.)*

RABBI: *Eil malei rachamim sho-khein bam'romim, hamm-tzei m'nukhah n'khonah tahat kanfei ha-sh'khinah, b'ma-alot k'doshim u-t'horimk'zohar ha-rakiya maz-hirim et nishmat Felix ben Chaim she-halakh l'olamo, b'gan eiden t'hei m'nuhato. Ana, ba-al ha-rahamim, hassti-rei-hu b'seiter k'nafekha l'olamim, u-tzror bi-tzror ha-hayim et nishmato, Adonai hu nahalato, v'yanu-ah b'shalom al mishkavo v'nomar amen.*

(Translation: *God of compassion, grant perfect peace in your sheltering presence, among the holy and the pure who shine in the brightness of the firmament, to the soul of our dear Felix Rosenbaum who has gone to his eternal rest. God of compassion, remember all his worthy deeds in the land of the living. May his soul be bound up in the bond of everlasting life. May God be his inheritance. May he rest in peace. And let us answer: Amen.)*

(GINNY *leaves* CHRIS *and joins* HENRY *by the grave.)*

GINNY: You're smiling.

HENRY: I am.

GINNY: You're happy?

HENRY: I'm happy. I'm standing here and Felix's dead—you're leaving, but still everything is perfectly clear.

GINNY: It is?

HENRY: Felix knew it. I know it. Some things are just true.

GINNY: Henry, I was wondering if you'd do something for me—my engagement ring.

HENRY: I'll look for it.

GINNY: I just feel awful, you know. How could I lose it? Will you keep a lookout for me? I feel like, if I just knew what happened—

HENRY: I'll find it.

GINNY: Henry, I promised Felix I'd do something—tell you something—but the thing is, I'm just...

HENRY: You're just married.

GINNY: Yes.

HENRY: You have a plane to catch.

GINNY: Goodbye, Henry.

HENRY: Goodbye, Ginny. Take care.

NOW + 12 WEEKS

(At the hospital. GINNY sits by FELIX's side. His face is gray with cancer. HENRY enters.)

GINNY: He can't see.

HENRY: Felix?

GINNY: He was fine this morning—we were talking— and then nothing. The doctors, they don't think...

HENRY: Felix, can you hear me?

FELIX: I'm blind, not deaf.

(HENRY *takes* FELIX's *hand.* GINNY *packs up her things.*)

GINNY: I'm glad you're here now. He needs you here. I mean, I'm going home soon and in a few weeks you'll be on your way to Europe.

HENRY: Without you.

GINNY: I can't stay. Chris is waiting.

FELIX: She's been avoiding you.

GINNY: I'm not avoiding him, my husband is waiting.

FELIX: It started two weeks ago—you've been avoiding him.

HENRY: It's true.

GINNY: I'm busy. We leave a week from Friday.

HENRY: That's not it.

FELIX: He's right.

GINNY: All right. Fine. Yes. Yes, I have. I'm sorry, Henry. I can't see you anymore.

HENRY: You can't see me?

GINNY: No.

HENRY: *(To* FELIX*)* She's breaking up with me. We're not even together and she's breaking up.

GINNY: Chris was upset. After you talked—the night of the presentation? He was upset.

HENRY: Chris? Chris was upset?

GINNY: Yes.

HENRY: Screw him. I'm upset.

GINNY: Henry, Felix is ill.

FELIX: I'm fine. You talk. Talking is good.

GINNY: *(To* HENRY*)* Look, I don't know what you said to him, but he doesn't want me to see you anymore.

HENRY: Is he your husband or your baby-sitter?

GINNY: What did you say to him?

HENRY: I told him he was stupid.

GINNY: You called him stupid.

HENRY: I told him he was stupid for taking you away—

GINNY: He's not taking me away. I'm going.

HENRY: And it's your choice not to see me anymore.

GINNY: He asked. I chose.

HENRY: You chose him.

GINNY: Yes.

*(*CHRIS *enters.)*

CHRIS: Everything all right in here?

HENRY: I guess I should leave you two alone.

*(*CHRIS *leaves.* HENRY *kisses* FELIX*'s cheek. As* HENRY *passes* GINNY*, she pulls him into a deep hug.)*

GINNY: You're going to be all right.

HENRY: No, I'm not.

*(*HENRY *leaves.* GINNY *sits by* FELIX*.)*

FELIX: I was right about you.

GINNY: They say you're dying.

FELIX: I am, I have it on good authority. It's not so bad. All those times you and Henry talk to me about science. You think I don't listen, but I do. Einstein. Relativity. I am dying? Meaningless. I have been dead a million years; I won't be born for another thousand. It depends on where you stand. I am. I am not. Time dances with us like a lover.

(GINNY *looks at her friend, lying on the edge of death's door. She takes* FELIX's *hand.*)

GINNY: Felix, I just want you to know how much I've enjoyed getting to know you—and that I think you are one of the most delightful souls I've ever—

FELIX: Again with this?

GINNY: What?

FELIX: We love you, Felix. We can't bear to be without you. Enough with this. You and Henry are about to lose the love of your life and you make speeches to me.

GINNY: Shhhhh. Felix—please. Chris's right outside.

FELIX: Your husband—I don't care about him. You don't either. It's O K. I know.

GINNY: Look, Felix—right now—it's not a good time to talk about this—

FELIX: You love Henry. You should tell him.

GINNY: Chris is right outside and—I'm confused—and it's just not a good time.

FELIX: I have a secret for you. The really big decisions in life aren't the ones that change the future. Changing the future is easy. The big ones come when we change the past—wait, didn't I tell you this before?

GINNY: Tell me what?

FELIX: Well, I told somebody.

GINNY: Shouldn't we be talking about something else? You're sick and somehow it's all about me.

FELIX: Me? No, I'm not such a big deal. I'm dying. Soon—all problems—over. You—your life is starting. You are the one with the problems.

GINNY: You know when this started? When I met you, I met you and then everything got strange. And now Chris—I'm leaving with him next week and I'm dreading it. I love him and I'm dreading it.

FELIX: It's going to be all right. Somewhere, somehow, it's going to be all right. I know. I've seen it.

NOW + 10 WEEKS

(Outside under the stars. GINNY *stands—trapped.* CHRIS *enters.)*

CHRIS: Ginny, there you are.

GINNY: Chris, what are you doing here? It's past midnight.

CHRIS: I've been looking everywhere. I thought maybe you were with Henry.

GINNY: He's not here yet.

CHRIS: Funny, isn't it? You weren't in your office, so the first place I think to go look for my wife is with Henry.

GINNY: He won't be here for a while.

CHRIS: I mean, that's the first place I look.

GINNY: He won't be here for another two years.

CHRIS: Seems like you're always with Henry.

GINNY: Not right now.

CHRIS: Ginny, I don't want you spending anymore time with him.

GINNY: What?

CHRIS: I just don't think it's a good idea.

GINNY: We've been working together.

CHRIS: But not anymore. You're done, right? Just don't see him anymore—please.

GINNY: Chris, honey, you're being ridiculous.

CHRIS: Am I? Good. I feel ridiculous. My wife spends every evening with another man and I'm sitting at home waiting for her like a fool.

GINNY: There's nothing going on.

CHRIS: He's in love with you.

GINNY: He just thinks he's in love with me. Look, the man's two shakes short of a rattle, right? He doesn't talk to people, he hides under furniture—I come along, I'm pleasant, I'm female, and I'm breathing. Hell, it's probably the first time he's had all that come together in one package—so of course I'm suddenly the love of his life. He'll get over it.

CHRIS: Will you get over it?

GINNY: What?

CHRIS: A few weeks we'll be back at home—for good. You spend all this time together—it's all you can talk about—

GINNY: Please. I'm married to you. I adore you. Me and Henry? It's just out of the question.

CHRIS: So it wouldn't bother you not to see him—

GINNY: He's a friend—

CHRIS: Ginny, can you honestly say to me that I have no cause for this? There's nothing between you and Henry. No threat?

(GINNY *doesn't answer.*)

CHRIS: I want to protect our marriage. Don't you?

GINNY: I won't see him anymore.

(CHRIS *wraps* GINNY *up in his arms.*)

CHRIS: You're the love of my life, Ginny. You are. It's all right. It's nothing. We'll be O K. We were together long before this whole thing and we'll be together long after.

GINNY: You think?

NOW + 9 WEEKS

(CHRIS *is gone.* GINNY *hasn't moved.* HENRY *enters.*)

GINNY: I am not going to Switzerland.

HENRY: You're upset.

GINNY: I am upset. What's wrong with me? I am very upset.

HENRY: You want to go?

GINNY: I don't know, it's my paper. The Haven Prize—do you know what that would do for my future in Physics?—If I had a future in Physics which I don't—definitely.

HENRY: But still—Switzerland.

GINNY: I hear they have good cheese.

HENRY: Great cheese. And chocolate. And Alps. They have Alps.

GINNY: Swiss cheese…Swiss Alps…

HENRY: You…me…

GINNY: And fifty thousand dollars.

HENRY: Hell yes.

GINNY: God, it sounds wonderful.

HENRY: And you said you were going home.

GINNY: I am going home.

HENRY: But the cheese and the chocolate and the Alps—

GINNY: God, things are so confused. And Chris—poor Chris—doesn't know what's wrong. I'm acting all off kilter and he doesn't know why. All he knows is that he wants to make it better.

HENRY: Does he know how brilliant you are?

GINNY: He has no idea.

HENRY: I do.

GINNY: You know what this is? It's pre-wedding jitters.

HENRY: You're already married.

GINNY: Then it's post-wedding jitters. I just feel like life is closing in—like maybe there's something I'm missing… Dancing.

HENRY: Dancing?

GINNY: You know—like Felix said.

HENRY: When?

GINNY: I don't know. It just popped into my head— BAM! Dancing. Something about dancing…

HENRY: When did Felix say this?

GINNY: I don't remember.

HENRY: All right then. Let's dance.

(HENRY *extends his hand to* GINNY's—*waiting.*)

GINNY: Look, I'm being—deranged. This is not a good idea.

HENRY: You don't know what you're missing.

(*Rising to the challenge,* GINNY *takes* HENRY's *hand. They laugh as they dance playfully underneath the stars.*)

HENRY: You know, it's too bad we didn't meet under that light bulb.

GINNY: Yeah.

NOW + 8 WEEKS

(At the podium. GINNY helps HENRY make a presentation to the High School Science Club.)

HENRY: So—the electron—it's either like in a kind of—well, in quantum mechanics—The Heisenberg Uncertainty Principle was first documented by—well—Heisenberg—

(GINNY steps in to rescue the nervous HENRY.)

GINNY: If an electron exists everywhere, but appears only when we look—the question is—how does it know which way to be? Right, Henry?

HENRY: Um—yes, right.

GINNY: Electrons are weird. Like a teacher.

HENRY: Like a teacher…or maybe a very smart college student.

(Looking at GINNY, HENRY suddenly regains his composure. He takes control of the lecture.)

HENRY: She might go on to a brilliant career. Or she might throw it all away and move to the backwoods of South Carolina.

GINNY: Henry—

HENRY: No, I think I'm getting the hang of this.

(HENRY forges ahead—confidently, passionately. In making his point to GINNY, he transforms from a nervous, shy neurotic guy into a strong, passionate, articulate speaker. TROUSANT sits in the back of the room—amazed.)

HENRY: *(To the group)* The point is, you don't know which way it is going to go. Neither does she. Yet.

GINNY: She knows. She definitely knows.

HENRY: Don't confuse the children, Ginny. *(To the group)* It turns out that, according to physics, there's no reason that quantum waves can't travel both directions in time.

GINNY: Look, the math is very complicated—

HENRY: I think they follow me. (*He draws an X on the blackboard.*) So, our young student is standing here. And she's sending out waves into the past and future. (*He draws a wave going forward from the X.*) "What am I? What am I?" she says. "Am I an electron that's going to be brilliant, way out there with energy and potential smeared out all over the place? Or am I going to be grounded and boring and spend the rest of my future with whisky sour and nice china and people with names like Muffy and Skip?"

GINNY: I drink mint julep.

HENRY: And these waves travel out around her, until somewhere out here—

(*To the right of the first X,* HENRY *draws another X on the board.*)

HENRY: Somewhere out here in the future, it meets another electron. This electron hears the question, "What am I? Do I belong at home with my feet locked down to the ground? Or do I belong out here?" So it takes a look. (*To* GINNY) It looks at her and it says, "I think it's obvious."

GINNY: (*To the students*) You should know that there's no way to prove any of this. It's just a theory.

(HENRY *draws a wave moving backward from the second X. The first wave and the second wave meet.*)

HENRY: And this interaction sends out another set of waves in both directions in time. The two waves cancel each other out everywhere in the universe except (*Pointing at the first X*) between this moment (*Pointing at the second X*) and this moment. So that it's not just the past that changes the future. It's the future that changes the past.

(FELIX *eats a Snickers bar in the back of the room. He raises it to* HENRY *in a toast.)*

(*Later in* HENRY's *office:* FELIX *and* GINNY *drink.)*

GINNY: I am calming down. Good. This sweaty panic thing—it is not attractive. *(She gulps down her drink.)*

FELIX: You like him, yes?

GINNY: We don't talk about it. No one is allowed to talk about it. It's just—I guess I just have this thing for a nice guy and a good science lecture.

FELIX: You should tell Henry this.

GINNY: No. It's ridiculous. I'm married. It will go away.

FELIX: Who wants it to go away?

(HENRY *returns.)*

FELIX: Time for me to leave you two alone.

GINNY: No, no—Felix—it's—

(Too late. FELIX *has gone.)*

HENRY: I was great tonight! I was fantastic! Me! Did you see Trousant? I thought he was going to fall out of his chair. It was amazing!

GINNY: I was amazed.

HENRY: I was nervous, and anxious, and terrified—and then, I suddenly wasn't. This is all because of you.

GINNY: You did everything, not me.

HENRY: Just wait 'till they hear us in Switzerland.

GINNY: Are you crazy?

HENRY: Yes. It's fabulous.

(CHRIS *enters.)*

CHRIS: Ginny, you told me nine o'clock. It's ten fifteen.

GINNY: Sorry about the time, sweetie. Henry and I got caught up.

CHRIS: Ah.

HENRY: We finished the paper.

GINNY: We're celebrating. Come on. Stay. Have a beer. You two should—I don't know—be friends.

(GINNY *thrusts a drink in his hands. She leaves to collect herself. Awkward silence*)

CHRIS: Are you sleeping with her?

HENRY: What?

CHRIS: You two have been spending a lot of time together.

HENRY: We've had a lot of work.

CHRIS: A lot of work. Every night.

HENRY: Yes.

CHRIS: I'd understand, you know. I'd forgive her. It'd be all right. In the end, it'd be all right. I just need to know.

HENRY: Ginny isn't sleeping with me—I'm not sleeping with her—nobody is sleeping with anybody.

CHRIS: She can't wait to go to work, she comes home late—I know what's going on—

HENRY: Physics. Physics is going on. We're physicists. Trust me, Ginny is completely, one hundred percent, maddeningly, irritatingly faithful to you.

CHRIS: She is.

HENRY: I hope you deserve it.

CHRIS: I'm sorry. I keep thinking about that day at lunch—what you said.

HENRY: We don't talk about it. It's her rule.

CHRIS: She never got like this before—always working. It's not like her.

HENRY: I guess she figures it's her last chance.

CHRIS: And you—you with all your fascinating insights about quarks and kryptons—I just let it—

HENRY: Leptons—

CHRIS: I don't like being talked to like I'm stupid.

HENRY: You are stupid.

CHRIS: I went to law school—top of my class.

HENRY: So you could get a job anywhere, do anything—and you drag Ginny all the way back to backwoods, South Carolina—

CHRIS: She wants to be there.

HENRY: She wants to be with you. You want to be there.

CHRIS: It's our home. We grew up there. I have an important job there.

HENRY: Ginny works on questions about the birth of the universe. What do you do for a living?

CHRIS: I don't have to answer to you.

HENRY: No you don't. Maybe you should talk to your wife.

(HENRY *gets up to leave.* GINNY *returns.*)

GINNY: Anything wrong?

HENRY: It's late. I should go.

GINNY: Come on, stay—we have to celebrate your triumph.

CHRIS: You heard the man, Ginny. He has to go.

GINNY: Henry?

HENRY: We'll catch up later.

GINNY: All right, then. Later.

(HENRY *leaves.)*

NOW + 2 WEEKS

(GINNY's *office.* GINNY *and* FELIX *crawl on the floor looking for something.* HENRY *flips through papers.)*

HENRY: Here, look at this—

GINNY: I can't.

HENRY: Look. They use the renormalization group equations to cut down the—

GINNY: Forget it. Stop. Not another word about Trousant's paper. Not until I find my ring.

FELIX: It'll turn up.

GINNY: I know I had it at the wedding. I remember that at least.

HENRY: I'm sure Chris will understand. He's perfect.

GINNY: This is my engagement ring.

FELIX: Yes.

GINNY: *(To* FELIX*)* Felix, you're not getting any ideas are you? Because I lost it?

FELIX: What ideas?

GINNY: Ideas about Henry and me.

HENRY: Felix already has plenty of ideas.

GINNY: *(To* HENRY*)* Look, I'm here because of the work.

HENRY: I know.

GINNY: I just don't want anybody to get any ideas.

HENRY: You afraid I might kiss you?

GINNY: Henry!

HENRY: I'm kidding.

(She grabs her books to storm out.)

GINNY: After that stunt you pulled last week, to sit there and—

HENRY: No. Ginny, stay. Please. I'm sorry. Ginny, it was a joke. It was a bad joke.

(GINNY stops.)

HENRY: Look, last week—I made things hard, I screwed things up, I know that—I'm sorry—but is this how it's going to be?

GINNY: You know when Chris proposed to me? First grade. I was six, he was nine. It was recess—some of the kids were teasing me, because they knew I was sweet on him. And I was crying, because Chris was standing right there and I was so embarrassed. But he didn't laugh. He came right up to me, got down on one knee and asked me to marry him. Right on the playground—the whole lower school looking on. Of course I said yes. Who wouldn't say yes? *(Sits)* Why can't I find my ring?

HENRY: Come on. I'll help you make some signs.

GINNY: Please.

NOW + 1 WEEK

(At a cafeteria table. GINNY and CHRIS hold hands.)

CHRIS: I'm telling you—a battle. With Emily Post's *Book of Etiquette* caught right in the crossfire.

(GINNY laughs. Completely ignoring CHRIS, HENRY steps up to GINNY.)

GINNY: *(To HENRY)* Hey, you want to join us?

HENRY: I'm in love with you.

GINNY: I'm sorry—pardon?

HENRY: I am completely obsessively in love with you.

CHRIS: Who the hell is this?

GINNY: Henry, this is my husband. I have a husband. This is Chris.

HENRY: Hi. I'm in love with your wife.

CHRIS: Ginny—

GINNY: *(To* CHRIS*)* We met last week.

HENRY: Yes—and then strange things started happening. I can't stop thinking about you. Me! I mean normally, I don't think about anything except math and the occasional sandwich, but ever since I've met you it's been all crazy with the hair, and the smile, and the scent of strawberries—what is that? Like a soap or a cream rinse or something?

GINNY: We met Tuesday.

HENRY: Oh my God, I'm acting crazy.

GINNY: Exactly.

HENRY: Weird, creepy, stalker kind of crazy.

GINNY: Yes.

HENRY: This is great! It feels great! Can you believe this? I am standing here, declaring my love to an almost complete stranger in front of her husband!

(CHRIS *slugs* HENRY. HENRY *drops to the ground.)*

GINNY: Chris! What the hell are you doing?

CHRIS: Me? What the hell is he doing?

GINNY: Let me take care of this.

CHRIS: He is out of line—way out of line.

GINNY: Go on out and simmer down before you hurt someone.

CHRIS: *(To* HENRY*)* Ginny is my wife. You remember that. *(Reluctantly, he leaves.)*

HENRY: I can see how he would be upset.

GINNY: Henry, what are you doing?

HENRY: I just had to tell you. That's all. I take it, maybe, you don't return the feelings?

GINNY: Henry, I'm married.

HENRY: You know how you meet someone—and you just know them—every word—every look? Well, I don't know how, but I know you. I know you're brilliant, I know you don't belong with him, I know there's a reason we ended up working together—

GINNY: Henry, no.

HENRY: No?

*(*GINNY *shakes her head.)*

HENRY: I sound like Felix, don't I?

GINNY: It's sweet. It's flattering. It's even romantic. But it's not real.

HENRY: The thing is, I've never felt saner in my whole life.

GINNY: Come on, let's get some ice for that thick head.

*(*GINNY *goes to get ice. Embarrassed, bleeding, disappointed,* HENRY *sits with his head in his hands.)*

NOW + 4 DAYS

*(*GINNY *walks across stage with a basket of laundry. She fumbles with car keys.* HENRY *enters with a shirt from his laundry—the same shirt that he was wearing in the first scene. He stops* GINNY.*)*

GINNY: Henry? What are you doing outside my apartment?

HENRY: I needed to speak to you. Alone.

GINNY: I'm on my way to do laundry.

HENRY: Perfect.

(HENRY *grabs* GINNY's *laundry basket and tears it open.*)

HENRY: Look, I think there are some very important issues that we need to figure the hell out— (*He makes a mess as he digs through the clothes.*)

GINNY: What are you doing?

HENRY: What were you wearing the other day?

GINNY: What?

HENRY: The day you got married. What were you wearing?

GINNY: Henry!

(HENRY *shows* GINNY *the shirt that he brought.*)

HENRY: Do you recognize this shirt?

GINNY: No.

HENRY: You've never seen this shirt before in your life?

GINNY: Is the shirt looking for an alibi?

HENRY: The Heisenberg Uncertainty Principle. I think we need to have a very important conversation about quantum non-locality and Heisenberg.

GINNY: The electron has a probability wave associated with—

HENRY: There is a coffee stain on my shirt.

GINNY: You are not making sense.

(HENRY *continues rummaging through* GINNY's *laundry. Unsuccessfully,* GINNY *picks up after him.*)

HENRY: Say we put something in a box—like, a cup of coffee.

GINNY: Isn't it supposed to be a cat? The experiment is called Schrödinger's cat.

HENRY: I'm doing it with a cup of coffee. *(A bra flies out of the bag.)*

GINNY: Would you please unhand my brassieres?

GINNY: We put a cup of coffee in a box, then say we make a gizmo that will knock the coffee over if it detects an electron. So if electrons exist everywhere *until* we look for them— Then physics says that the coffee must be *both* spilled all over the place *and* sitting in the cup until we look in the box to find out.

GINNY: Henry! What is the matter with you?

(HENRY finds a blouse in the bottom of the bag. The same blouse that GINNY was wearing in the first scene. There is a coffee stain all over the front.)

HENRY: There's a coffee stain on your shirt.

GINNY: This one? How? *(She examines the shirt.)*

HENRY: I don't know how. But Felix has this whole story about how I met you under a burnt-out light bulb and you spilled coffee all over the front of my shirt— this shirt.

GINNY: We met in the atrium.

HENRY: Not according to Felix.

GINNY: You are getting yourself all worked up over a couple of laundry stains.

HENRY: He thinks we're destined for each other—

GINNY: I'm not destined for anybody except my husband.

HENRY: You don't think it's strange?

GINNY: Felix is a sweet, crazy man with a brain tumor. Just relax. I mean, I'm married. I married Chris. In front of God and a preacher and two witnesses. *(Falls silent)*

HENRY: Look, Ginny. I have had the weirdest couple of days.

GINNY: I know.

HENRY: You do?

GINNY: We just have to forget about it.

HENRY: What about the coffee?

GINNY: It didn't happen. We were there. We'd remember. It didn't happen.

HENRY: Right.

NOW + 1 DAY

(HENRY and GINNY sit in the hospital room. FELIX lies in bed.)

GINNY: God, a brain tumor. I am so sorry—

HENRY: Your husband's probably worried—

GINNY: I called. He'll be all right.

HENRY: This is nice of you—not many people would sit at the hospital all day with a complete stranger.

GINNY: *(Checking watch)* Fourteen hours, we're not strangers any more.

HENRY: I guess not.

(GINNY offers HENRY her hand.)

GINNY: Here.

HENRY: What's that?

GINNY: My hand. I thought you might want to hold my hand.

HENRY: For what?

GINNY: Some people like it. It's a Southern thing. Somebody's upset, you hold their hand—that and you bake something.

(Very tentatively, HENRY *takes* GINNY's *hand.)*

HENRY: You bake something?

GINNY: You know—bundt cake, cinnamon bread, sometimes a peach cobbler—

HENRY: Mmmmm. You hungry?

GINNY: I'm O K.

HENRY: Come on. They have vending machines. I'll buy you some Fig Newtons.

*(*GINNY *and* HENRY *stop and look at each other.)*

GINNY: How'd you know I like Fig Newtons?

HENRY: I don't know. *(Something strikes him.)* You love Fig Newtons. You dunk them in skim milk.

GINNY: We met this morning.

HENRY: I don't know, I just got this flash.

GINNY: Please.

HENRY: Well, it's strange, isn't it? Fig Newtons—what are the odds?

GINNY: Lots of people like Fig Newtons.

HENRY: Come on, you do me.

GINNY: We just met.

HENRY: Go on. Close your eyes. Extend your senses—

GINNY: You put gin in your coffee.

*(*HENRY *stops cold.)*

GINNY: Like you said—a flash.

HENRY: O K, that's it.

GINNY: Coffee and gin?

HENRY: A bad habit from college—

GINNY: I'm sure it was just a lucky guess.

HENRY: Sure.

GINNY: Try this—what am I thinking right now?

(HENRY *sneaks a look at the book she carries.*)

HENRY: Something about Dark Matter Candidates in Astrophysics.

(*This spooks* GINNY.)

HENRY: I saw your book.

GINNY: Oh, you! I read one of your pieces in the journal—I was going to try to meet you. I wanted to work on a paper together.

HENRY: You're an experimentalist. You're not even an experimentalist, you're an undergrad.

GINNY: Doesn't mean I can't read.

HENRY: You dabble in theoretical physics.

GINNY: I was doing research. I had an idea for this paper—

HENRY: I don't usually do collaborations.

GINNY: You don't have to usually do it, you just have to do it now. "Dark Matter Candidates: Theory versus Experiment." I think we should work together.

HENRY: I think we have to.

GINNY: You do?

HENRY: I don't know, I just got this flash—

(FELIX *wakes up.*)

FELIX: Henry?

GINNY: You want me to stay?

HENRY: Please.

(FELIX *smiles when he sees* GINNY.)

FELIX: It's her.

NOW

(CHRIS *leads* GINNY *to her cubicle.* GINNY *notices the* MINISTER.)

GINNY: Who's he?

CHRIS: That's better.

MINISTER: Reverend John Hawkins.

GINNY: Who?

MINISTER: Many thanks. Your fiancé got me straight out of a deacon's meeting.

GINNY: You're a Minister?

CHRIS: What do you say we get married, Ginny?

GINNY: I say it's a good idea. I just sent out the invitations.

CHRIS: What do you say we get married now?

GINNY: Now?

CHRIS: I can't wait three months. Let's go, just you, me, and the hijacked Minister.

GINNY: Chris, I don't know.

CHRIS: What do you mean you don't know?

GINNY: I'm busy with this project—

CHRIS: You're going to put off the man of your dreams for a bunch of little bitty specks?

(GINNY *doesn't smile.*)

GINNY: They're called leptons.

CHRIS: But do they have my good looks, my Southern charm?

GINNY: Chris, this is really just sudden—

CHRIS: It's not sudden, Ginny. We've been engaged for a year—

MINISTER: Maybe I should leave?

CHRIS: Stay. Ginny, what's there to think about here?

GINNY: Nothing, I just thought I'd have more time— I've been busy.

CHRIS: Too busy for us? Go on, now—let me pull one of those lepton pictures up on the computer. You tell me if it's more exciting than your fiancé.

MINISTER: I could just wait—

CHRIS: It's fine, Reverend.

GINNY: It's not a picture, it's more like a splat.

CHRIS: Whatever it is, if it's better than me sweeping you off your feet, I'll go home.

(CHRIS *clicks on an image. It appears on the large screen.*)

CHRIS: What do you think?

(GINNY *stares at the graph. The colors explode out from the center like fireworks.*)

GINNY: God, look at those jets.

CHRIS: Ginny—

GINNY: This could be something.

CHRIS: Like what?

GINNY: I mean it might be just background noise, but look at that high-energy electron—and the muon....

CHRIS: Ginny, I got on a plane and came all the way up here to have a wedding.

GINNY: The accelerator produces millions of collisions every second. Do you know what the odds are against seeing something like this?

CHRIS: Better than the odds of you marrying me?

GINNY: And you—just pulling it up at random— Millions to one. Billions to one.

CHRIS: Come on. What are we waiting for? Let's do this thing.

GINNY: Are you listening to me? This is important. It's unique.

CHRIS: This is work.

GINNY: There are millions of collisions a second, billions a day, and we look hoping to find the one that's unique, exotic. *(Looking at the screen)* And it does happen, we exhaust every possibility and we find the ones that gives us a glimpse into the nature of the universe.

CHRIS: In three months, you and I will be back home in South Carolina and none of this will make any difference.

(GINNY looks at him in a sudden moment of complete clarity.)

GINNY: I can't marry you.

CHRIS: What?

GINNY: I can't marry you. *(She begins to cry.)*

CHRIS: Oh, sugar, of course you can. It's all right.

GINNY: No, it's not all right.

MINISTER: I should go. *(He flees.)*

CHRIS: *(To the* MINISTER*)* Wait. *(To* GINNY*)*
You're overwhelmed—that's all. Marriage, it's
overwhelming—come on—you want to wait three
months? We'll wait.

*(*GINNY *takes off her engagement ring and gives it to*
CHRIS*.)*

GINNY: You should take your ring.

CHRIS: Now, Ginny, just calm down now—you're not
thinking clearly.

GINNY: All of a sudden, I am thinking very clearly.

CHRIS: Ginny, what has gotten into you?

GINNY: I'm sorry, Chris—No. *(Upset, she runs away.)*

CHRIS: Ginny! Come back here! Ginny!

*(*CHRIS *throws the ring in the trash can—the same spot
where* FELIX *found it in ACT ONE.)*

(Across the stage. FELIX *and* HENRY *stand underneath the
burnt-out light bulb.)*

FELIX: You believe me. Why else would you put up
with me?

HENRY: What do you want, a candy bar?

FELIX: Snickers.

*(*HENRY *gives* FELIX *a Snickers bar.)*

FELIX: Maybe she's pretty.

HENRY: She's fictitious. I know I'm desperate, but I
draw the line at dating imaginary women.

FELIX: Pretty. And smart—she's very smart. You like
that.

HENRY: Destiny doesn't happen in hallways.

FELIX: Sure. Down the hall from the fire extinguisher,
under the burnt-out bulb. Destiny has to happen
somewhere.

(HENRY *pours himself a cup of coffee from his Thermos. He adds a shot of gin. He checks his watch.*)

HENRY: Almost nine.

(*They wait in the silent hallway.*)

FELIX: Today, I think. Definitely today.

(FELIX *tries to stand. He gets dizzy and leans against* HENRY.)

HENRY: Felix, you O K?

(HENRY *holds* FELIX *and his Thermos. At that moment—* GINNY *rounds the corner. Upset and crying, she does not see* FELIX *and* HENRY. *BAM! She runs into* HENRY *right underneath the burned-out light bulb. She spills coffee all over their clothes.*)

GINNY: Oh God! I'm sorry! I'm so sorry—I just—I didn't see—

(FELIX *smiles with delight.*)

HENRY: Are you all right?

GINNY: I'm um—I think I just destroyed my future.

FELIX: It's her.

GINNY: Who?

HENRY: Felix, you still dizzy?

FELIX: No, no. I'm fine. I'll just let you two…

(FELIX *steps back and watches them as if he were watching a wonderful romantic movie.* HENRY *pulls a napkin from his bag.*)

HENRY: Here, you need this?

GINNY: Thank you. I am so sorry about your shirt.

HENRY: It's all right.

GINNY: It's going to be stained.

HENRY: Plaid. Who can tell?

GINNY: Cold water. Soak it overnight.

(HENRY *notices* GINNY'*s tears.*)

HENRY: Are you crying?

GINNY: *(Cleaning her face)* Oh. Right.

HENRY: Woah, hey, don't cry. It's just a shirt.

GINNY: No. It's not that. I just had a bad… It's not you.

HENRY: You're sure? It's not me? When people are upset, it's usually me.

GINNY: I think maybe I'm losing my mind. I just did something really stupid—or maybe really brilliant—I don't know.

HENRY: Ah. It's going to be all right.

GINNY: How do you know?

HENRY: I don't. But it sounds good.

FELIX: You see how it goes.

HENRY: Felix— *(To* GINNY*)* This is my friend, Felix. I'm Henry.

GINNY: Hello, I'm Ginny.

FELIX: It's her.

GINNY: *(To* HENRY*)* It's me? What's me?

HENRY: Nothing.

GINNY: God, things are so confused. I just need everything to slow down—slow down and stop for a second.

(HENRY *pulls the roller skates out of his bag.*)

HENRY: Here, you need to borrow these.

GINNY: Roller skates?

HENRY: Relativity. Move fast enough and the rest of the world slows down.

GINNY: You're going ten miles an hour.

HENRY: O K, so it doesn't slow down by much.

TROUSANT: *(O S)* Henry!

HENRY: In fact, I'll go with you.

(At HENRY's *signal,* FELIX *leaves to stall* TROUSANT.*)*

GINNY: Now?

HENRY: No time like the present.

GINNY: You don't have somewhere you need to be?

TROUSANT: *(O S)* Hennnnnry!

HENRY: Not really.

GINNY: Henry…Henry Rainer? Oh God! I've been wanting to meet you. I read your paper. The one in the journal—it was a great paper—

HENRY: Let's talk about this outside.

GINNY: Dark Matter Candidates. They're working on that in Italy, you know. Everyone has the problem of getting—

TROUSANT: *(O S)* Henry!

GINNY: You're sure this is a good idea?

HENRY: It's a great idea.

*(*FELIX *returns with a ladder.* HENRY *leads* GINNY *off the stage.)*

GINNY: *(O S)* Everyone has the problem of getting the electronics sensitive enough to reduce the background noise, but they've made improvements—

HENRY: *(O S)* You're an experimentalist?

GINNY: *(O S)* Not even. I'm an undergrad.

HENRY: *(O S)* What are you doing reading my papers?

*(*TROUSANT *enters.)*

TROUSANT: *(Seeing* FELIX*)* Have you seen Henry Rainer?

FELIX: *(Pointing in opposite direction)* I think he went that way.

TROUSANT: Henry!!

*(*TROUSANT *leaves, following* FELIX'*s direction. Humming,* FELIX *climbs the ladder.)*

FELIX: *(Singing)* Ba-da-da-da-daaa-da-da da. Mmm-hmmm-mmm-hmmm-mmmm-hmmm-mmmm.

(The clarinet music from the airport scene comes in over FELIX'*s voice. It blends perfectly with the tune. The violin music from the first scene joins in. The sounds blend together.* FELIX *takes a light bulb from his pocket. He unscrews the burnt-out bulb and puts in the new one. He smiles as the light goes on.)*

END OF PLAY

www.ingramcontent.com/pod-product-compliance
Lightning Source LLC
Chambersburg PA
CBHW052202090426
42741CB00010B/2379